KNITTING WITHOUT NEEDLES

KNITTING
without
NEEDLES

By PEGGY BOEHM

Illustrated by SHIZU MATSUDA

CORNERSTONE LIBRARY   New York

Reprinted 1964

This new Cornerstone Library edition is published by arrangement with Sterling Publishing Co., Inc. and is a complete and unabridged reprint of the original hardcover edition.

The publisher wishes to thank Deitra Carpenter for her assistance in rendering the drawings.

CORNERSTONE LIBRARY PUBLICATIONS

Are Distributed By
Affiliated Publishers
A Division of Pocket Books, Inc.
Rockefeller Center
630 Fifth Avenue, New York 20, N.Y.

Manufactured in the United States of America
under the supervision of
Rolls Offset Printing Co., Inc., N.Y.

CONTENTS

BEFORE YOU BEGIN

Sometimes half the fun of making things is having people exclaim, "Don't tell me you made *that* yourself!" Especially is this true when the "that" is something odd, and interesting—the kind of thing you can "knit without needles." After all, knitting with needles is something that most people can do, one way or another, and even the machines nowadays are able to do a first-rate job. But once you throw away your needles, it's a bit like throwing away your oars. To get the boat back to shore, you have to dream up ways that are sure to be ingenious!

Ingenious and fun to make! Those are the hallmarks of the many clever and practical things you can make out of yarn (or even string) in ways other than needle-knitting or crocheting. Knotting and twisting and tying can turn hanks of yarn, or even just odds and ends of left-over yarn, into amazing items for use in the home, or to wear, or to play with. Most of them are so simple that even very young children will be able to do them, and the projects lend themselves well to groups at camp or club or school. By the same token, even the simplest projects will suggest to the more experienced craftswoman a sophisticated version using the same techniques.

Included is a chapter on weaving, based on units of a small square woven on a simple little frame, and this chapter is a case in point. The lovely lightweight afghan may seem a far cry from dolly's little blanket, but it is in reality only a larger version of it!

Tapestry is another art worked with wool, a fascinating pastime as well as a practical way of bringing beauty into many articles useful in daily life. In the tapestry chapter, for each project (explained so simply that anyone can do it) you will think of several others you will want to work out on your own.

The chapters on toys to make, play clothes and real clothes include some hilarious suggestions as well as many practical ones. Some are of the hurry-up variety, so that you can make them on the spur of the moment: If the immediate appeal of sporting purple hair strikes you to the core, for example, you can make yourself a purple wig almost before you can say Jack Robinson.

A word about the materials you will use: Often these are mere scraps and left-overs of yarn or floss, or bits of string saved from bundles and packages. Sometimes you need a whole new hank of yarn. However, it doesn't really matter, in any of these projects, just what kind of yarn you use. There are so very many different kinds of yarn on the market that their variety is often bewildering, but whether you use so-called "fingering yarn" or Shetland floss, or afghan yarn or a thinner or thicker yarn matters hardly at all.

Occasionally you may want a nice thick yarn when you have only thin yarn on hand, but you can easily figure out what to do about it. For instance, when the directions for a fat black tassel tell you to take 15 turns and you find that 15 turns of your particular yarn make a skimpy tassel, it's easy to give it another 5 or 10 turns,

8

isn't it? If you decide you want the tassels on the whirly skirt closer together—or farther apart—you can merely rearrange the intervals to please yourself. It isn't like a pattern for a sweater which will come out with one sleeve at the hip instead of the shoulder if you don't count stitches accurately! It's all fun and frolic, but you will end up with many worthwhile concoctions, gifts, items of merchandise for a bazaar, and conversation pieces to intrigue your friends.

I. For the House

YARN BUBBLES

Suspend a group of delicate yarn bubbles from a doorway or ceiling in your home and friends will exclaim with delight, never dreaming that you made them yourself! They do look like fairies' handiwork, but they are easy and interesting to make.

To begin with, make about a quart of wallpaper paste or a thin, runny flour-and-water paste in a basin or bucket. Then soak 10 to 15 yards of cotton yarn or any soft, absorbent string in the mixture until it is wetted through.

Next you need a toy balloon. Blow it up, knot the end and tie on a long piece of string. Start wrapping the wet yarn or string around the balloon, turning and twisting it in all directions. When the balloon is covered with a nice network of string, hang it up from a chandelier or a hook in a doorway and let it hang undisturbed overnight, or until the string is thoroughly dry. As it dries, the string will stiffen and hold its shape. To complete the bubble, puncture the balloon with a pin or needle. When it has collapsed, carefully remove it through the largest space. The string will maintain the shape of the balloon in lacy loveliness.

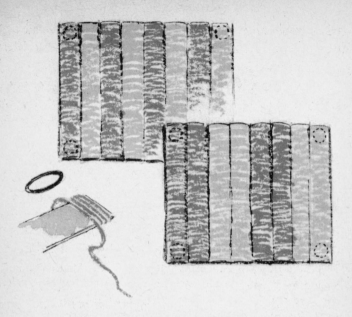

TWO-TONE BEDSIDE RUG

A warm, woolly rug alongside your bed will feel good under your feet, especially if you have made it yourself. You will need two hanks of heavy yarn, in two different tones, but select dark shades that will not soil easily, since this rug is not washable.

Cut some heavy cardboard or corrugated paper board into eight strips, each $4'' \times 12''$. Twist the darker yarn around four of the strips and the second shade around the remaining four. Wrap the yarn evenly, covering the entire cardboard, then wrap each cardboard a *second* time, for added thickness and warmth.

When you have finished wrapping the eight sections for the second time, assemble them according to either illustration. Thread a large darning needle with the darker yarn and whip-stitch the sections together. Be sure to wear a thimble, but sew rather loosely. If you pull the yarn too tight, your rug will not lie flat.

Sew a rubber jar ring to each of the four corners on the underside of the rug. They will prevent the rug from slipping when you step out of bed on to it.

WALK-THROUGH ROOM DIVIDER

To make two small rooms out of one larger room usually involves the mess of building a wall, and some loss of light and air. A clever—and handsome—solution to the problem is a walk-through room divider made of woollen yarn and wooden beads. It is a big project but an enjoyable one, and it lends itself well to family or group participation. The result will be a truly worthwhile accomplishment.

The room divider consists of free-hanging strands of woollen yarn. They are suspended from a wooden strip or lath fastened to the ceiling of the room at half-inch or one-inch intervals. (If the ceiling is very high, you may prefer to hang the strands from a wooden beam or pole attached to opposite walls at below-ceiling height.) The strands of yarn are strung with wooden beads at intervals so that the overall result is either a geometric pattern or a random effect.

Air and light will be able to circulate freely through this room divider, and so will you! There are no doors to open or close, and you can walk through at any point as easily as a ghost going through a wall in a spooky film.

To get started, first prepare the room for the divider. Hammering carefully so as not to crack the plaster, attach a wooden strip to the ceiling. Paint the strip to match the ceiling. Measure the length of the strip to find out how many strands you will need. Figure one strand to the inch for a rather "sheer" wall, two to the inch for a denser wall. Measure the distance from ceiling to floor to find out how long to make each strand.

Designing the room divider will give lots of scope to

your creative and imaginative powers. Do you want to use beads of natural wood? Or wood which has been waxed? Or stained? Have you a collection of wooden spools you can use instead of beads?

Do you want brightly enamelled beads, in shades to match or contrast with the yarn? Do you want to use beads of only one shape or many shapes? Would you like to experiment with acorns or dried berries? Perhaps you have a collection of seashells which you chose especially because each one had a little hole at its apex, ideal for stringing!

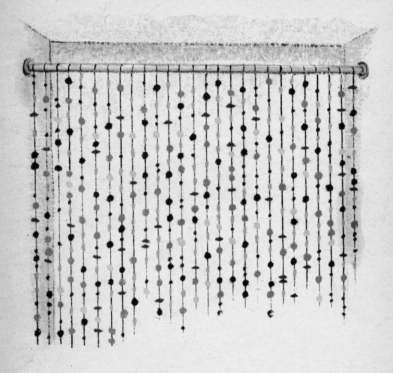

How about the pattern? Do you want to work out an intricate geometric pattern? Would you like a checkerboard effect? A simple random scattering of beads? Work out a few ideas on graph paper and then experiment with the actual yarn and beads. String several strands with beads and lay them on the table, or suspend them from a coat hanger, to study the effect. You will, of course, note that the closer together you place the beads, the more solid your wall will appear—and the more beads you will use.

Once you have decided on the pattern, you will be able to figure out how many beads you will need. You may also have to work out just how to keep the beads in place. If they fit snugly enough over the yarn, they will stay put with no additional help from you. However, if they are a little too loose, you may be able to keep them in place by wedging each bead with a small length of wooden matchstick or toothpick.

An extremely attractive way to keep the beads in place is to make a knot directly below each bead. Even if you do not really need the knots, you may decide that the effect is worth the extra work involved. To find out just how long each strand must be so that it will come out right when knotted, bead and knot a sample strand.

A random pattern is particularly suitable when you intend to make a knot below each bead. Start by making a knot at the bottom of the strand. Slip on a bead from the other end and then make another knot a few inches above it. String another bead, add another knot, and so on, ending with a knot at the top of the strand.

You can wait until you have completed the necessary number of strands before hanging them from the wooden strip on the ceiling. Or, if storing the finished strands is a problem, you can tack them in place each time you have completed a batch. Use small carpet tacks and a light tack hammer. Be sure to hammer through the knot at the end of each strand.

You will be pleased by the attractiveness and usefulness of this versatile kind of "wall."

WINDOW CURTAIN

Here is a novel window curtain you can make out of yarn and bits of sipping straws. The procedure is the same as for making the room divider, but you tie the strands to a string or curtain rod at the top of the window, or the top of the lower sash. However, you can tack them directly to the window frame, if you prefer. This window curtain is light and airy, and it rustles delightfully in a breeze.

Measure the height and breadth of the window. Allow six strands of yarn for each inch of breadth. For instance, if the window is 30" wide, you will need 180 strands. Each strand must be as long as the window is high, or longer if you wish the curtain to hang below.

You will need a package or two of drinking straws. You can use either the kind which is manufactured of paper or the kind made of real straw. You may even be able to make your own if there is a swampy place available where you can pick thin reeds. Snip the straws into lengths of from 1" to 3" according to the design you plan to use. You can make them uniform in size or vary them. (If your scissors flatten the ends of the straws, roll them gently between thumb and forefinger to restore roundness.)

The simplest way to make the window curtain is to cover each strand of yarn completely with snips of straws. You can also place the little pieces of straw at intervals to form a pattern. This is easy if they fit snugly over the yarn, or you can keep each piece of straw in place by knotting the yarn, as for the room divider. Since the bits of straws are light, they will not weigh down the yarn, and the knots will give a slightly zig-zag effect which is quite pleasing.

Experiment to find the pattern you like best, either by using actual yarn and straw or by first working out a design with paper and crayons.

2. Very Simple

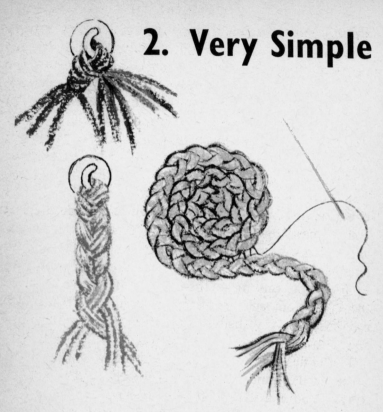

BRAID-A-HOT-PLATE

There is something primitive and elemental about making a braid, and something rather mysterious in the way our fingers seem to know just how to go about it. Here is a good way for a little girl to learn to make braids, and at the same time to braid a hot-plate to protect the dining table from hot dishes. You can use up odds and ends of different yarn, either cotton or wool, unless you want your hot-plate a special color.

Take 9 strands of yarn about 10 feet long and knot

all the ends together. Divide the bundle into 3 triple strands of yarn and make a rather tight braid. You can catch the knot on a hook or perhaps a drawer pull to make it easier to braid. When you have finished the braid, knot or tie the end. Coil the braid into a flat round, sewing it in place with needle and thread. If you want a large hot-plate, untie the end knot and tie a new length of yarn to the end of each strand. Continue braiding and sewing until the Braid-a-Hot-Plate is the size you need.

Tuck the knotted ends between the braids, as you coil, and sew them out of sight.

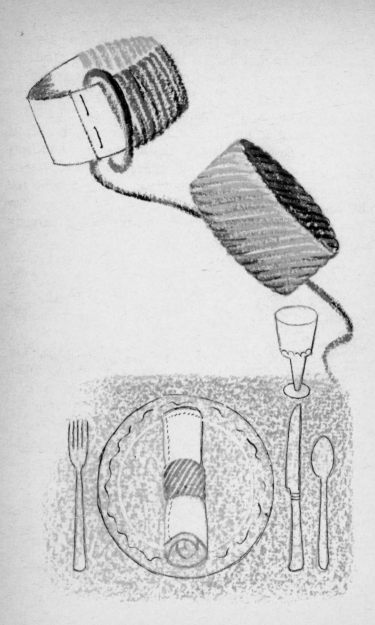

RAINBOW NAPKIN RINGS

The pot of gold at the end of your rainbow may only be a bowl of carrots, but you can dress up the dinner table with a whole rainbow of napkin rings. Make a red ring for the oldest member of the family, orange for the next oldest, then yellow, and so on round the rainbow according to age.

To make each napkin ring, cut out a strip of flexible cardboard 1″ × 6″ in size. If the cardboard is too stiff, work it gently over the edge of a table until you can shape it into a ring, then glue or staple the ends together firmly.

Now start winding yarn in and out of the napkin ring, taking care to turn the strands neatly in one direction. You can wind them straight up and down or in a slanting direction, but keep them even and cover every bit of the cardboard. When you have finished, fasten the two ends of yarn tightly and tuck them in, out of sight.

SKATING HAT

Here is a hat you can knot together from a single hank of yarn. Cut the yarn through once and open it out. Grasp the two cut ends and knot the hank in the middle with a single loose knot.

Now cut a piece of elastic or a strip of felt to fit your head and sew the ends together for a hatband. Next, start tying the cut ends of the yarn to the elastic. Take a few strands at a time, twist them once around the elastic and then knot the ends around it. Continue working around the hat until you have tied all the yarn ends to the hatband.

This makes a warm, attractive hat for skating or sledding. If you wish, you can sew a few little silver bells to the knot or top, so the hat will tinkle every time you move your head. This hat would make a wonderful Christmas gift.

OVAL PICTURE FRAME

An oval frame will enhance any picture you place in it. To get a perfect oval, take a piece of paper 2″ longer and 2″ wider than the photograph. Fold it in quarters, open it, and then draw one segment of the oval as shown in the diagram. Now trace the second part of the first half of the oval. Fold the paper the other way and trace the other half. This is the inner edge of the oval frame.

Make the frame 1″ wide by drawing a second oval 1″ outside the first. Now cut out the frame and trace its outline 3 times on to heavy cardboard. Cut and glue these 3 cardboard frames together.

Starting at the top of the oval, wind a layer of yarn closely around the frame to cover up the cardboard. After you have gone around once, continue winding until you complete a second layer of yarn. Keep the

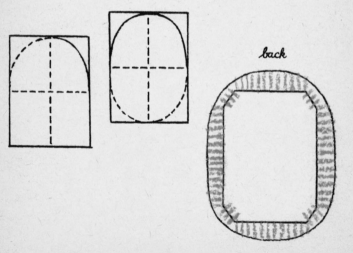

back

twists of yarn smooth and even as you work. Finish by knotting a double loop of yarn at the top for hanging.

Before framing your picture, trim its corners, if necessary, so that they won't show. With a sharp needle and thread, tack the picture to the back of the frame by stitching down the 4 corners.

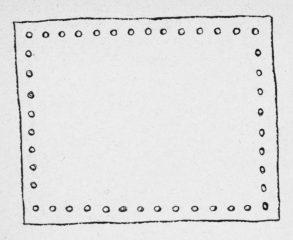

EASY PLACE MATS

Shirt cardboards and odds and ends of yarn may not sound like much to start with, but from these simple left-overs you can make very attractive place mats to use at mealtimes.

Here's how to do it. First, punch holes all around a shirt cardboard, one inch apart and one inch in from the edge. Thread a strand of yarn through a darning needle, and sew slanting stitches (whip-stitch) through the holes. When you have stitched around the mat completely in one direction, change the color of your yarn, reverse your direction, and stitch around again in the opposite direction. Your stitches, too, will go in the *opposite* direction, making a pretty border.

Next take a long stitch from the left-hand hole on the top, to the second hole from the left on the bottom. Then stitch under the mat to the first left-hand hole on the bottom and up to the second hole on top. Continue this X pattern completely across the mat. To finish, make a horizontal row of stitches across the mat, sewing *through* the cardboard and catching the crosspoint of each X.

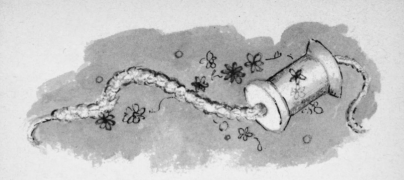

SPOOL KNITTING

If you have never knitted with a spool, you should try your hand at it now. There's a soothing, almost hypnotizing quality about working around the spool and watching the knitted rope grow. This rope is sometimes called a "horse rein," no doubt because it was used that way many years ago. Certainly it is strong and flexible enough for that purpose!

You can buy a knitting spool in almost any toy or craft shop, or you can make one yourself in a matter of minutes. Take an empty wooden spool and firmly hammer five U-shaped tacks around the top according to the illustration. Some people prefer a spool studded with carpet tacks instead of U-tacks. One advantage of carpet tacks is that the yarn cannot slip off as you work, but the stitches are slightly harder to knit. However, a crochet hook helps a lot.

In spool knitting you knit around the top of the spool and as the rope forms, it goes through the hole in the spool and trails out of the bottom. To start knitting, run the loose end of a ball or length of yarn through the spool until a few inches emerge at the bottom.

Make a slipknot in the yarn above the spool and slip it over one of the little wickets or tacks. Carry the yarn around the wickets counterclockwise (unless you are left-handed) in a complete circle. When you get back to the slipknot, pass it over the new strand from outside to inside. Use a pointed wooden stick or a crochet hook to work with. Carry the yarn around the next wicket and again pass the lower loop over the new one, and over the wicket, to the inside. Keep on working, round and round the spool, giving the rope a little tug from the bottom every now and then, as it emerges. You can use up odd bits of yarn by piecing them together as you work, or you can even work with pieces of string instead of yarn.

THINGS TO MAKE
WITH SPOOL-KNIT HORSE REINS

OVAL RUG: Fold a 12″ length of horse rein in half and sew it together. Coil the horse rein around this and continue coiling and sewing it together until your rug is the desired size—or until you use up the horse rein!

HOT PLATE: Coil the horse rein into a flat round about 6″ in diameter and sew it together.

BERET: Start this hat by making a flat round, as for the hot plate, and then decrease the circles until the edge of the hat measures your head size.

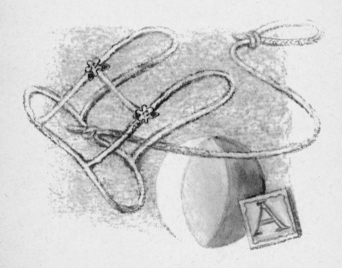

BABY HARNESS: Keep baby in tow with a harness which goes around his waist and over his shoulders, with long ends for Mother to hang onto.

BELT: Draw a soft rope through a length of horse rein measuring 30″ longer than your waistline. Make a single knot at each end and tie the belt around your waist.

LUGGAGE IDENTIFIER: See page 111, and use instead of braid.

DECORATION: Since the horse rein is in reality a hollow tube, you can run a soft rope through it for stuffing to make it rounder and thicker. Use it to trim the edge of a coat or jacket.

3. Toys to Make

WOOL PUPPETS

Hand puppets are pals when there is no one to play with, and can serve as actors when you want to put on a show.

An old ball of yarn that has been wound too tightly for reuse makes a perfect base for a simple stick puppet, or you can wind a new one. Then all you have to do is embroider on a pair of eyes and eyebrows, a nose and a mouth. You can add a fringe of hair or braids, if you wish, or make a little hat out of paper or cloth. Push the head on to the end of a stick and you have a fine stick puppet!

To make a more elaborate hand puppet, start with the same kind of head and add a little dress or coat to cover your hand. Cut out two pieces of cloth according to the pattern shown here and sew up the seams.

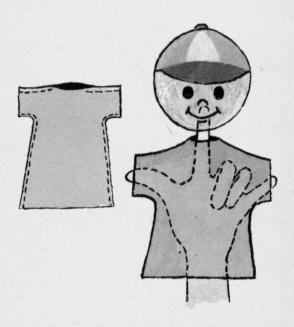

Put the finished coat over your hand with your thumb in one of the arms and your little finger in the other. Your index finger goes through the neck. Poke a hole in the head and slide it down over your index finger and you are ready to begin the show! (See Vernon Howard's *Puppet and Pantomime Plays*).

BUNNY BALL

A wonderful toy for a young baby is a soft woolly bunny made of balls of yarn in pastel shades. Bulky, new yarn is best, especially if you intend to give this as a gift, but used yarn will also make a nice bunny for baby to play with.

For bunny's body, wind a ball of yarn firmly, but not too tightly, until it is 4″ in diameter. Use a darning needle to sew the end of the yarn into the ball, so it will not unravel. This is an important step for each of the balls which make up the bunny.

Now make a 1½″ ball for the bunny's head. For the

ears, begin by wrapping the yarn around your three fingers about 10 or 15 times, to form a core, and then twist the yarn around the core to form a bunny ear. Make two. Make three 1″ balls—two for the hind legs and one for the tail. (This bunny manages quite well without front paws.)

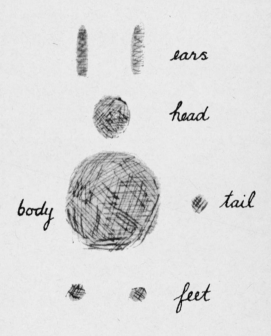

ears

head

body tail

feet

Assemble the balls, as shown, and sew them together securely. Finish the bunny by embroidering on his eyes, nose and a few teeth, and embroider the inside of the bunny's ears, in pink.

MR. OCTOPUS

Mr. Octopus is pink. Who ever heard of a *pink* octopus? Well, now *you* did!

To make Mr. Octopus, you need a hank of heavy pink cotton yarn and a styrofoam ball, about 3″ in diameter. A rubber ball or an old tennis ball will do; so will a tightly-wound ball of yarn you have no further use for. (Perhaps you unravelled an old sweater but never got around to reusing the yarn!)

Clip through the hank of new cotton yarn and tie one cut end tightly together with a piece of yarn. Now drape that tied end over the ball so that none of the ball shows

through. Pull the yarn tight around the ball and tie it just below Mr. O's head.

Divide the dangling yarn into 8 separate bundles and braid each bundle.

Tie each braided "leg" with black yarn about 1″ from the end. Make a double knot and then tie a small bow to trim the leg.

Twist several loops of black yarn around Mr. Octopus' neck, ending with another bow. Embroider large, sad eyes of black yarn, then add a single stitch of white yarn to finish up each eye with a glint. One more black bow on the top of his head completes Mr. Octopus.

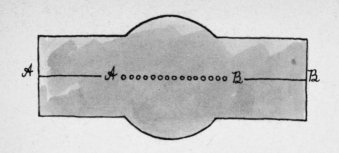

YARN BALL

Babies and small children love a roly-poly ball to play with, and when it comes to tossing and catching, there is nothing like a feathery-soft yarn ball to learn with. A child will not flinch when a soft, woolly yarn ball comes at him, for he knows that it cannot hurt him even if it lands in his face instead of his hands.

To make the ball, first take a piece of stiff cardboard and cut out a form as pictured here. The circle should

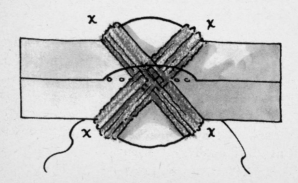

be about 3″ in diameter. Cut slots along lines A-A and B-B and use a needle to perforate a line of little holes from A to B.

Start winding the yarn diagonally in two directions. You will need about 200 twists, but switch from one direction to the other every 10 twists.

Lay a piece of strong, soft twine across the yarn and pull the ends through the slots. Turn the whole thing

over and tie the ends in a single knot, pulling steadily and hard enough so that the string tears right through the perforations. Tie just as tightly as you can and knot the string securely several times.

With a pair of large shears cut the yarn through at the four corners marked "X." Remove the cardboard pieces and fluff up the ball. If it is not perfectly round you can trim it to shape with your scissors.

4. Dress Up and Play

WOOLLY WIG

Children love to dress up and pretend they are someone else. Best of all is to change the appearance of their hair. Even adults sometimes find themselves in need of a wig for a masquerade or theatrical performance. Here is one made easily out of a hank of yarn. Use wool in a natural hair shade if you are aiming for reality— well, let's say an approach to reality. Or, make a really "mad" play wig of bright green, perhaps, or purple yarn!

Start with a 6″ circle of felt or canvas or cut up an old, unwanted hat. Felt, straw or any fabric will do. Cut off a shallow portion of the crown and discard the lower part. Open the hank of yarn and cut it through at both ends, giving you two bundles. Lay one-half from left to right across the hat top. With a large darning needle and a length of yarn, stitch down this "side hair" with a row of stitches running from front to back, like a part

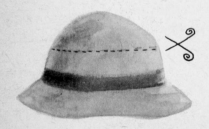

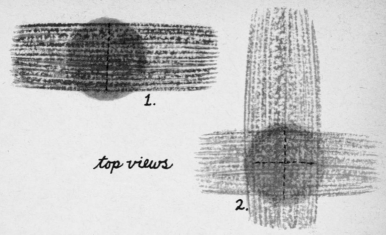

top views

1.

2.

down the middle. Now lay the rest of the yarn across the wig at right angles to the first half. You can place it far enough back to form bangs, or let it hang down long in front. Spread it so that it hangs evenly and then sew it on with a row of stitches running crosswise.

To "dress" the wig you can give it a haircut or trim, part it, braid it into one or two pigtails, or pin it up in an "upsweep." Tie it on to your head with a gay ribbon or a bandeau, or pin it in place with hairpins and surprise your friends.

45

HULA SKIRT

A hula skirt will delight any little girl who likes to dress up and make believe. To make the skirt, you will need an old belt, or a ribbon, or a strip of cloth, or tape or an elasticized band for the waistband. Anything that you can fasten about the waist will do. The skirt itself consists of yarn, string or raffia, or all three.

This is another good way to use up left-over odds

and ends of unmatching yarn. You can combine different types of yarn, of any weight or color, and mix in string or cotton twine. Real hula skirts are made of raffia, so if you have any on hand, by all means use it, too. It will make the skirt rustle when the wearer moves about.

To find out how much material you will need, measure the waist size and the distance from the waistline to the top of the knee. For every inch of waistline you will need 20 strands of yarn, each *twice as long* as the skirt length.

To make the skirt, all you have to do is to knot or tie the middle of each strand of yarn or raffia to the waistband. Or, if you have a lot of short strands you want to use up, you can tie them by an end. Trim the skirt with scissors to even off the bottom.

FUZZY FEZ

Here's a dress-up item which little boys will love. It is a wonderful hat to wear for marching in a parade.

Make a cylinder of cardboard or buckram which will

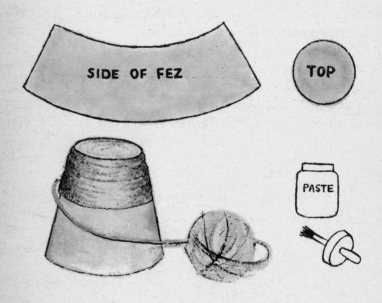

fit around the head comfortably. It should be about 6″ high. Fasten the ends together at the bottom edge by poking staples through both thicknesses and flattening the ends. Shape the fez by making the top narrower than the bottom, and then fasten the top with another staple. Trim off excess cardboard at top and bottom. Cover the cardboard or buckram with paste, and then

twist red yarn round and round until you have covered the entire fez. Next add bands of bright yellow or gold-colored yarn at the top and bottom of the fez.

Attach a black tassel to the top edge of the fez. This is the front of the hat. (See page 61 for instructions on making a tassel.)

5. Things to Wear

PENCIL FLOWERS

Here is an unusual way to create bright nosegays of wool flowers. Each flower takes only two short pieces of yarn, one 24″ and the other 12″ in length, and you make the flower by wrapping the yarn around a pencil.

Lay the short length of yarn along the pencil, and twist the long piece around both pencil and yarn in an even spiral. Do not pull the yarn tight as you wind. Next, push the spiral together, and start to knot the loose ends of the short piece of yarn. They will form the stem of the flower. Slide the whole flower off the pencil carefully, holding the spiral loosely in shape, and pull

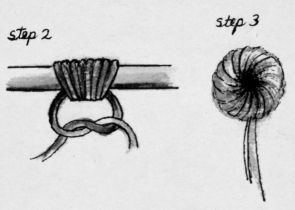

step 2

step 3

step 1

the stem tight, completing a double knot. Your flower is finished!

Make 12 or more flowers for each nosegay, tie the stems together and trim the ends. Add a small safety pin and the nosegay is ready to wear. You can make the flowers all of one color, or in different harmonizing shades of a color. Make the stems to match, or make them look more realistic by using green yarn. An attractive wildflower nosegay consists of red, yellow and blue flowers with bright green stems.

A nosegay of pencil flowers will perk up a collar, belt or handbag. Flowers make lovely gifts in themselves, or can be added to another gift as an "extra bonus" in trimming the package. And these pencil flowers, colorful and different, will sell like hotcakes at a church or school bazaar.

GRETCHEN HAT

For a little girl who does not have pigtails of her own, there is nothing nicer than a Gretchen hat. Here is how to make one:

Cut a rectangle of white felt measuring 6″ × 12″ and embroider all around the edges with red yarn. Use a blanket stitch, working the stitches a half-inch apart

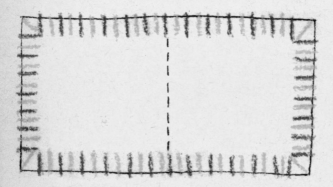

and a half-inch deep. When you have finished all four sides, start again with bright green yarn. Make the

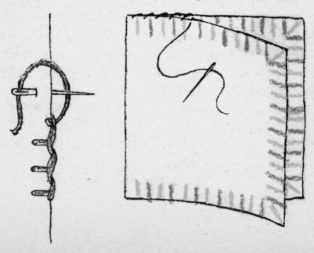

green stitches the same size as before, but work them midway between the red stitches.

Now fold the rectangle in half and whip-stitch one side together, starting at the fold. This will be the top of the hat, and the fold will be in back.

For the Gretchen braids, open a hank of yellow yarn and cut it through at each end, giving you two bundles of yarn. Divide each bundle into three parts and braid a fat pigtail out of each bundle. Tie the bottom end of one braid with a bow of red yarn, one inch from the tip, and tie the other braid with green yarn.

Stitch the tops of the braids to the inside of the bottom edge of the hat, one at each side. They will hang over the wearer's ears and keep them warm on frosty days. You can also sew on an elastic band to go under the little girl's chin to keep the hat in place.

TICKLE-TOE BOOTIES

Take a whole flock of woolly tassels, place the knotted sides down and the fuzzy sides up, and make them into cold-weather booties for your pet toddler. An elastic band connecting all four corners of the oversized "sole" holds the bootie on the child's foot.

Measure the length and the width of the child's foot and add an inch to each measurement. This will give

the size of the sole, a rectangle which you will form out of tassels. Allow three tassels to the running inch in each direction. For instance, if the child's foot measures $2'' \times 4''$, the rectangle will measure $3'' \times 5''$, or 9 tassels by 15 tassels. That means 135 tassels for each bootie.

Make the tassels according to the directions on page 61, winding the yarn 15 times around a one-inch cardboard. Use the same piece of yarn with which you tie the loop at the top for twisting around the loop. Knot it well and cut the loop open at the other end to form the fringe.

String the tassels together in rows by sewing them through their heads. In the example given above, you would make 9 rows of 15 tassels each. Line up the rows

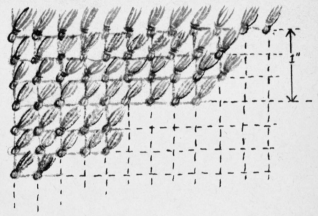

and sew through them at right-angles, according to the illustration. To complete the slippers, make circlets of elastic and sew them to the four corners.

The novelty of these booties will amuse small tots, and the fact that there is no "right foot" and "left foot" will encourage them to don the slippers instead of walking around barefoot on cold, drafty floors.

OLD-HAT HANDBAG

There probably is not a household in the land without at least one battered old felt hat hidden away in a cupboard or attic, which no one will ever wear again. Here is a way to make something new and useful out of something old and useless. A slice from the crown of the hat will be the base of a basket-weave pocketbook.

Cut about 33 or 35 strands of heavy yarn, each 20" long. Use a sharp darning needle to thread each strand through the edge of the felt shell, at $\frac{1}{2}$" intervals, and about $\frac{1}{4}$" in from the edge. Knot each strand at its midpoint with a single knot. Continue sewing and knotting the strand around the edge at $\frac{1}{2}$" intervals. Be sure to end with an odd number of strands.

Attach the loose end of a ball of yarn to one edge of the felt. A thick, bulking yarn is best for this purpose. Now start weaving round and round, as you would weave a basket. Do not separate the original strands, but work them in pairs. Since the yarn is not stiff, like the reeds of a basket, you will find it easiest to work the handbag upside down. To do this, sew a temporary strand of yarn through the top of the crown and suspend it from a coat hanger above a table so that the ends of the hanging strands just reach the table. Place a cylindrical box, or a cylinder made from a piece of cardboard, on the table inside your work so that the handbag will hold its shape as you weave.

When you have woven 5″, knot the yarn to one of the strands so it will not unravel, and cut it off. Separate

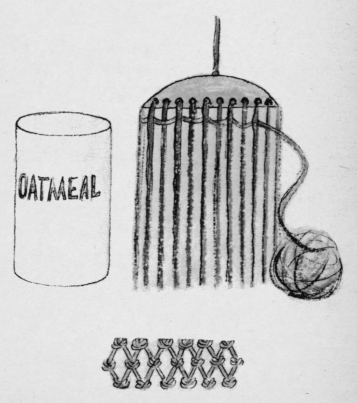

the pairs of strands and tie one strand of each pair to the adjacent strand, as in fringing, where the weaving ends. Next, knot the extreme ends of the hanging strands together in pairs. Finally, string a double circle of yarn, 48″ long, through the ends of the pairs of strands for a draw string. Before you knot the draw string, slip on two large beads and knot them in place at opposite sides, as in the illustration, and the bag is complete.

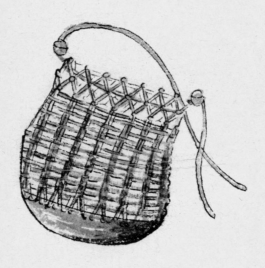

TERRIFIC TURBAN

Do you yearn to be a dazzling blond? Would you like to be a temporary redhead? Or have you thought how amusing it might be to sport a head of green or pink "hair"? This turban may turn your head—a different color. It will also keep your head warm, and if necessary, hide a multitude of curlers.

To make the turban you need a hank of wool or cotton yarn in whatever color you desire, and a net cap with an elastic edging. You can make the net cap

59

yourself from a circle of net, gauze or sheer cotton about 15″ to 18″ in diameter.

Stuff the cap with a pillow or crumpled tissue paper or newspaper to give it a rounded head shape. Open

out the hank of yarn, which is already tied once, and tie it a second time at the opposite side. Drape the whole hank around the cap in loops and waves and puffs and folds. Try to cover every bit of the cap. Sew the

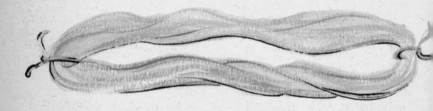

yarn to the cap in loose stitches, using matching thread or yarn and taking care not to sew through the pillow.

Teen-agers especially will find many occasions when they want to cover pincurls or rollers, or hide unset hair temporarily, with this terrific turban.

6. Tassels and Fringe

TASSEL PULLS

You can make any number of things with tassels that are useful in themselves or as ornamental trimmings for larger items. Tassels make attractive window shade pulls or lamp pulls, and have the added virtue of being noiseless. They do not click against the window pane or lamp base.

To make a tassel, wind 12 turns of yarn around a

broomstick or around three of your fingers or a piece of cardboard. Then slide the yarn off and slip another piece of yarn (about 24″ long) through the circle. Tie this length of yarn at its mid-point with a firm knot. Then take a short length of yarn and wrap it around the tassel 3 or 4 times, $\frac{1}{4}″$ below the knot. Tie a tight knot and trim the ends. Cut open the other end of the circle with scissors and you have a tassel, complete with pull.

Adjusting the size of the tassel is easy. You can make a longer tassel simply by wrapping the yarn around a wider cylinder, or all 5 of your fingers, or a wider piece of cardboard. You can make the tassel fuller and fluffier by taking more turns of the yarn.

TASSEL DOLLS

Once you find out how much fun it is to make a tassel doll, you will want to make whole families of them. You can make tiny tassel dolls to wear as decorations, or larger ones that are big enough to play with.

LAPEL OR NECKLACE DOLLS

Twist thick yarn around three of your fingers about 12 or 15 times. Remove the loop and tie it with a single strand of yarn. Let it hang by that strand (which is at the top of the doll's head) and pull the loop down. Now form the head by tying the dolly's neck with a few

turns of yarn, according to the illustration. Cut the loop open at the bottom, and you are ready to turn the tassel into a girl doll.

Cut a few strands on each side to form the doll's arms, and tie each arm at the wrist. Now cut away the outer strands of yarn, midway between the end of the arms and the very bottom, for the doll's skirt. Divide

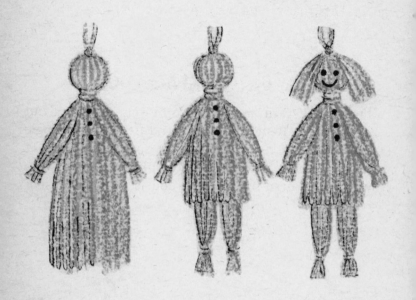

the remaining long strands into two bundles and tie each bundle at the ankle. You can also tie the knees, if you care to. Now your dolly has legs.

For a finishing touch, embroider eyes, nose and mouth. Insert a small safety pin at the back of her head, and dolly is ready to pin on your dress or coat. Or you can leave the yarn tied at the top of dolly's head long enough to wear around your neck as a necklace.

BOY DOLLS

To make a boy doll, you start exactly as you did for the girl doll and continue until you have completed the arms. Next, tie the boy doll around the waist, and divide all the strands below the waist into two, for the legs. Tie each leg at the ankle. You can twist a length of yarn around the leg to give the effect of tight pants, or leave the pants baggy like a little Dutch boy's. Give your boy eyes, nose and a mouth, and he is finished.

PLAY DOLLIES

A large play dolly made of yarn is a lovable toy for a baby or small child. It is soft and safe and cuddly, an ideal toy to go to sleep with.

Instead of a tassel made around your finger, you will need a whole skein or hank of yarn. Open out the hank into a large loop and tie the loop for the top of the doll's head. Tie the neck a few inches below, just as you did for the tiny dolls, but insert a small ball of yarn inside the head to give it more roundness. Push the neck up tight and the head will hold its shape and not lose its stuffing.

When you cut off yarn for the arms, braid each arm

down to the wrist and then tie it firmly. Tie the doll's waist with a thin braid of yarn for either a girl doll or a boy doll. Cut a skirt for a girl doll, and then braid the legs before you tie the ankles. For a boy doll, simply start braiding each leg a little below the waist.

Sew on features and hair, too, if you like. You can dress the girl doll in doll clothes instead of cutting her skirt out of the yarn itself. Just make her like the boy doll to begin with, and then dress her like a girl.

FRINGE-BENEFIT PLACE MATS

For each of these place mats you will need a rectangle of burlap or canvas cloth measuring about 12″ by 16″ and some embroidery floss in matching or harmonizing colors for the fringe.

Hem the long ends (top and bottom edges) of the mat with a narrow hem and baste or pin a hem in the narrow ends (the sides). Use a ruler to measure off half-inch intervals for the fringe along the narrow ends of the mat and place a pencil dot at each place, according to the illustration.

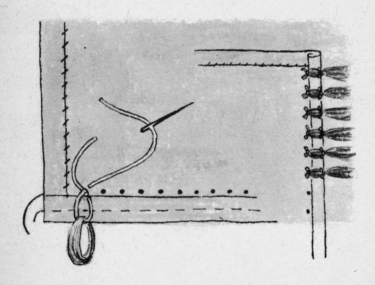

Cut a strip of heavy cardboard $1\frac{1}{2}''$ wide and wind the embroidery floss around it, making 6 turns. Slide off the loop. With another length of yarn sew the loop to the mat at the first pencil dot with two stitches, and then twist it around the loop a few times, ending with a tight, strong knot.

Continue until you have fringed both ends of your place mat. Remove the basting stitches or the pins, and then cut through each loop to finish the fringe. If the fringe doesn't look quite even enough, or if you would like to make it shorter, trim it with sharp scissors.

POM-POM STOLE

A stole is a welcome addition to almost any wardrobe and makes a wonderful gift. You will need a rectangle of some loosely-woven wool or synthetic fabric or jersey, about 20″ wide by 60″ long. The wool for the fringe can match the stole, but black fringe is more striking in appearance and practical as well.

Hem all four sides of the stole, either by hand or machine, with a narrow hem. If the material is fuzzy enough so that it will not unravel, you can leave the long sides unhemmed and simply hem the two short ends where the fringe will go.

Mark the places for the fringe tassels at one-inch intervals across the hems at each end, using pencil dots or straight pins. Thread a length of yarn through a tapestry or embroidery needle and pull four short lengths of 6″ each through the first dot according to the illustration. Tie the ends and pull them tight. After you have tied all the knots, trim them evenly across the stole.

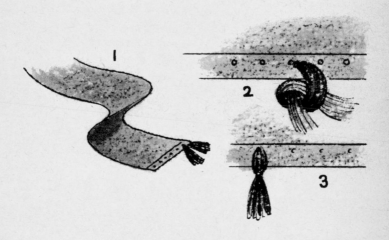

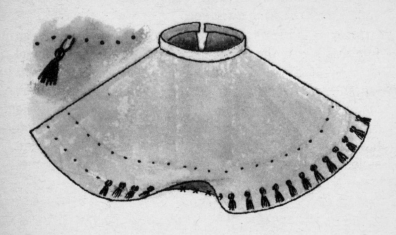

WHIRLY SKIRT

Circular skirts are becoming to all girls, thin and chubby alike, and they never go out of style. This whirly skirt is particularly pretty. It is made of felt, an easy fabric to work with, trimmed with a double row of black tassels.

You can make a circular skirt up to 16″ in length (from waist to bottom edge) from one square yard of felt. For a skirt of that size, cut a circle 36″ in diameter out of wrapping paper to use as a pattern. Or you can make a compass by tying a piece of string around a stick of chalk. Make a knot exactly 18″ from the chalk. Find the mid-point of the piece of felt by folding it twice, open flat, hold the knot there and, keeping the string taut, trace a circle with the chalk.

Whether you use pattern or chalk, cut out the felt circle carefully so that you obtain a clean, even edge, for this will be the bottom edge of the skirt. It is not necessary to hem felt.

For the waistline, fold the circle in half and mark the mid-point of the fold. For a waist of 18″ to 19″ cut an oval opening 6″ long at the fold. An easy way to find out just how big to make the oval for the waist is to tie a string around the girl's waist and then lay the string

chalk

on the table in an oval shape. The waistline should be 1″ longer than the actual measurement, for an overlap. Just remember not to cut away too much, for you can always make the waist larger by cutting away felt, just as you can make the skirt shorter by trimming the bottom edge.

Stitch on a waistband of felt, according to the illustration, allowing for overlap of the waistband itself. Add hooks and eyes, or a button and buttonhole. The skirt closes in back, and the plaquet is simply a 3″ slit which will overlap itself because of the extra inch of waistband.

Lay the skirt out flat and mark a chalk circle 3″ up from the bottom edge, then another circle 2″ above that. With chalk mark or pins, mark the spot for the thick, fluffy tassels of black yarn at 2″ intervals. (The chalk circles and marks will brush off easily afterwards, but if you use a rather dark felt, it will be better to use the chalk on the wrong side.)

Make the tassels by winding the yarn around a one-inch piece of cardboard, taking 15 turns for each tassel. Slide the loop off and complete the tassel according to

directions on page 61. However, do not trim off the ends of the yarn at the top of the tassel, as you will use them to attach the tassel to the skirt. Using a tapestry or embroidery needle, poke first one dangling end and then the other end through the felt skirt from front to back. Space the threads $\frac{1}{8}''$ apart from each other, and tie them together on the reverse side with a secure knot.

CATCH-ALL STRING BAG

There are many uses for an attractive string bag. You can use it for balls of yarn or twine; as a shopping bag for small purchases; to carry books or tennis balls; or to hang in the closet for mittens in winter. It is handy to carry about, too. It fits easily into purse or pocket, for it takes up almost no space when it is empty, even though it can stretch to hold a surprising amount when necessary.

The bag is made of pieces of string and lots of knots.

You will need 18 strands of soft but sturdy cotton string, each 36″ long. Make a bundle of the strands and join them all by tying the bundle securely at the mid-point. Then fold them at that point. You now have 36 loose ends.

Take two of the strands and knot them together 2″ from the joining point. Continue knotting the loose strands two at a time until you have made 18 knots, each 2″ from the mid-point. Lay the work out on a table, spreading the 18 double strands into a sunburst. Next,

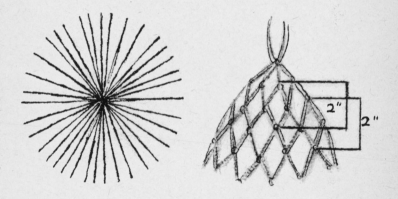

take a single strand and knot it to one strand from the adjacent pair, 2″ away from the previous knot. Knot the odd strand to one strand from the next pair, and continue all round until you have 18 knots in this row. Make a third row of knots in the same manner, again separating each bundle of two, and tying adjacent pairs to each other.

In order to keep your work from slipping, you may find it helpful to put a cloth on the table, or to weight down the work by placing a heavy object on it. Another way to work is to suspend the string bag from the central knot so that the strands hang down vertically.

When you have tied 10 rows of knots, divide the remaining strands into two bundles. Divide one bundle into three parts and braid it. Then braid the other, so that you have two braids, one on each side. Tie the braids together near their ends to form the handle of the bag.

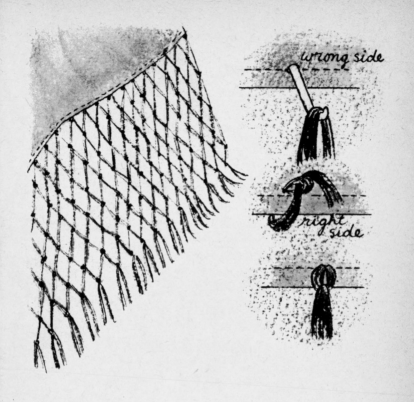

wrong side

right side

A SPANISH SHAWL

Be a merry señorita and tie the boys in knots when you wear this flirty Spanish shawl with a broad fringe all around it. Start with a 30″ square of brightly patterned silk or rayon, or use a pretty kerchief of about that size. Sew a narrow hem on the sewing machine or hand roll the hem of the square. For the fringe you can use either silk or a silky cotton embroidery floss.

To start the fringe, cut 3 strands of floss to a length of 36″ and then fold them in half. Draw the loop through the silk square from back to front just above the hem, using a crochet hook. When the loop is large enough, pull the ends through it. Tighten. Repeat around all 4 sides at 2″ intervals.

If you prefer a triangular shawl, start with a square of 36″ or even larger. Cut it in half diagonally. Hem all three sides, but put fringe on the two short sides only.

Now follow the same directions as for knotting the shopping bag on page 76. However, since you are working with triple strands here, you will be tying 3 strands from one bundle to 3 strands of the adjacent bundle. Make 6 rows of knots, keeping them evenly lined up. You will have about 6″ of fringe hanging free at the bottom.

You can, if you wish, make a heavier fringe by doubling the number of strands to start with. Place the strands one inch apart and knot them at one-inch intervals for an even finer Spanish shawl.

7. Tapestry

HOW TO EMBROIDER TAPESTRY

Tapestry embroidery is a creative art form which has been practiced for literally thousands of years. It is enjoyable handiwork with a repetitious stitch which is soothing and satisfying, and patterns which are easy to follow and fun to work out. Even simple geometric designs such as checkerboard effects, stripes, diagonals and diamonds are effective in a tapestry.

Tapestry is embroidered on to a special canvas woven in a mesh of strong linen threads. A special tapestry needle is used, with a large eye and rather blunt point. The needle carries the yarn through the holes of the mesh,

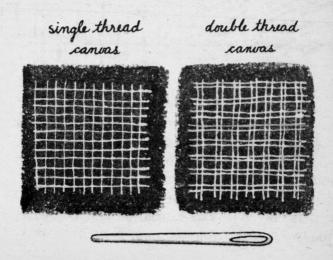

single thread canvas

double thread canvas

entering each hole twice and forming compact rows of diagonal stitches. When the tapestry is completed, the canvas is covered altogether and the fabric appears to be made entirely of the wool yarn you have embroidered with.

There are two ways of working tapestry, both of which are illustrated here. The first method gives an extremely strong, durable fabric—one that will with-

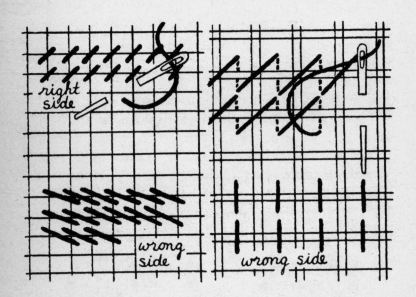

stand years and years of hard wear. Chairs and footstools are often covered with this type of tapestry. The second method takes the same amount of time to work, but it requires less yarn. It is perfectly suitable for any project in this book, and you probably won't care a bit if it lasts only 200 years instead of 300! Use whichever of the two methods you find most pleasant to work.

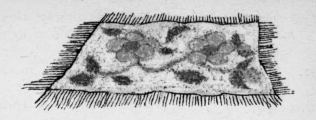

BLOCKING TAPESTRY

You will discover as you work your tapestry that a piece which started out as a rectangle changes shape and becomes a parallelogram. After you have finished embroidering your tapestry, a good blocking will restore its shape and give it a finished look. It is possible to

have a tapestry blocked professionally, but it is not difficult to do it yourself, and it takes only a few minutes.

Place the tapestry face down on a well-padded ironing
board and pin down one edge with rust-proof pins $\frac{1}{2}''$
or $\frac{1}{4}''$ apart. Now stretch and coax the piece into the shape
it is supposed to be, pinning it down as you work. Slant
all the pins outward, so that you will be able to get at
your work with the iron.

Set the iron a little hotter than the usual adjustment
for wool. Place a clean, dry cloth over the tapestry and
on top of that place a clean wet cloth. Press down lightly
with the iron. Repeat this several times, wetting the
cloth each time, and each time pressing a bit harder. A
steam iron may be used instead of the wet cloths.

After the tapestry has been thoroughly steamed and
pressed, leave it pinned down to the ironing board until
it is completely dry. If it does not hold its shape
properly when you remove it, block it again.

EYEGLASS CASE

A tapestry eyeglass case makes a thoughtful gift for someone who wears glasses. It is especially nice for the sort of person who is constantly taking her glasses off and putting them on again, for it protects the lenses from scratches.

Take a piece of canvas 7″ square and plan a design for half of the square. You can use simple stripes, diagonals or a series of borders, or a geometric design based on triangles, or design tall initials to march boldly across the face of the eyeglass case. Count the number of meshes per inch and multiply by 7 and by $3\frac{1}{2}$. A 10-mesh canvas, for example, would give you 70×35. Draw a checkerboard of that size, or use graph paper, to work out your design beforehand. The back of the case can be worked plain in a solid color.

When the tapestry is complete, block it according to the directions on page 83. Turn under the canvas edges

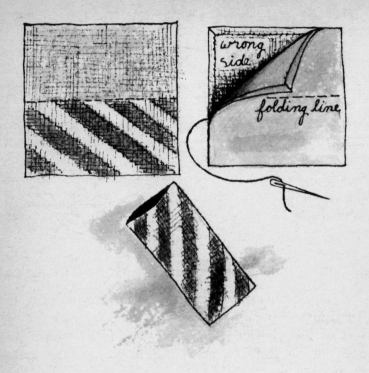

and baste them. Line the square with silk or satin or felt, or a smooth cotton fabric such as sateen or chintz. Then fold the case in half and sew two sides together, the long side and one end. Steam-press the case flat as the finishing touch.

CROSS-STITCH TAPESTRY BOOKMARK

Anyone who loves books will welcome a bookmark to mark his place without damaging the book. Make a number of these pretty tapestry bookmarks to have on hand for casual giving—to send off to a friend in a letter, to take to a convalescent, or to a hostess; to give to a friendly teacher, or to donate to a bazaar.

Choose canvas with 12 meshes to the inch. Your finished work will measure 1″ × 6″, but it is easier to work on a larger piece of canvas and cut it out afterwards. Also, it is helpful but not essential to use an embroidery hoop, if you have one. Instead of wool, use 3 strands of 6-strand embroidery floss. (It is easy to separate.) This embroidery is worked in a cross-stitch, which means that after you work the diagonals in one direction, you go over the work a second time making diagonals in the opposite direction. Counting out your stitches, follow the pattern given here.

This bookmark has dark blue for a background, light blue for half the flowers and pink for the others. The

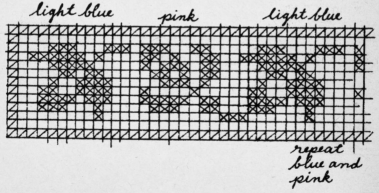

single-row border is of light blue. It is mounted on a matching light blue ribbon. Of course, you can choose any three colors which please you. Or, you can use only two colors, working all the flowers in one color and the background in a harmonizing color.

To mount the completed embroidery, block it first (see page 83) and then turn under the edges and baste them. Hem the tapestry to a 12″ length of grosgrain ribbon, 1½″ wide. Turn under the end of the ribbon, mitering the corners as illustrated. With sharp scissors, fork the other end of the ribbon and the bookmark is finished.

A GIFT OF TIME

Calendars for the New Year make splendid Christmas gifts, and you will find them especially helpful for the "difficult" names on your list. You may find that you can solve half your problems with this clever gift, which is guaranteed to keep you in mind for at least a year.

Buy small calendars in advance, as you will need to know their exact size. They should be about 1″×2″. You can find them at any stationer's, and they should cost only a few pennies each. Some of them come already gummed, ready to be stuck into place.

For each calendar you will need coarse canvas measuring approximately 5″×7″. The finished plaque should measure about 4″×6″, but you may have to make it larger to accommodate your calendar. Place the calendar in position according to the illustration and trace around it in soft pencil or ink. Working the diagonal tapestry

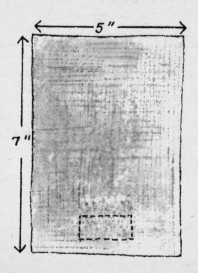

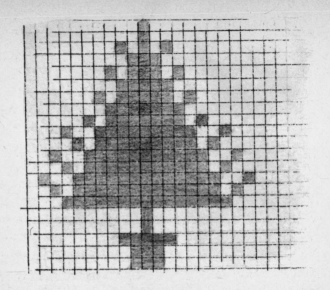

stitch described on page 81, embroider the tree in green yarn, counting out the stitches. If your calendar is large, you may want to place the tree to the left and embroider your initials, or even two pairs of initials ("A.B. to C.D.")

to the right. Then work the background in red yarn, omitting the space for the calendar.

Block the finished piece (see page 83) and turn under the edges, hemming them or gluing them in place with rubber cement. Cut a piece of strong paper or light cardboard slightly smaller than the plaque for backing. It should be big enough to cover the turned-under edges, but it must not show from the front. Cover the backing with rubber cement and spread rubber cement over the back of the plaque. Let them both dry somewhat, then press them firmly together. Glue the calendar into the place you have left for it, either with its own glue or using rubber cement in the above manner. Lastly, sew a small loop to the top of the calendar for hanging.

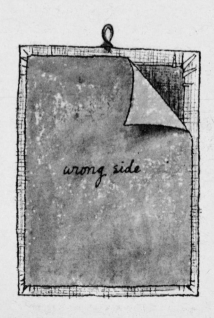

wrong side

LANDSCAPE HANDBAG

Here is a type of tapestry work in which you take stitches of varying lengths, instead of going into every hole. This kind of tapestry lends itself well to pictures and scenes, such as a lovely landscape. It works out well, too, in simple geometric designs and patterns which you may design, and if you are really artistic, you can even adapt paintings by the masters, such as a street scene by Utrillo or a Japanese scene. The actual embroidery is interesting, and it goes fast.

To make a clutch handbag measuring 5″×8″ you will need a piece of coarse canvas mesh 9″×15″. You can use the colors suggested here or others of your own choosing.

The stitches run from top to bottom and can be worked in either of the two methods shown here. Use tapestry yarn or Shetland floss, and follow the pattern.

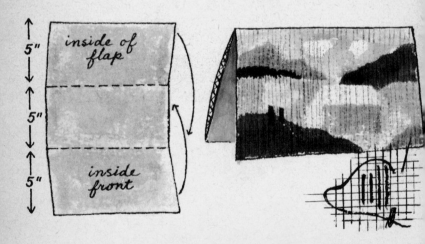

When the work is finished, block it (see page 83) and then line it, following the instructions for lining the eyeglass case on page 85.

Fold the work up from the bottom at the indicated line and whip-stitch the sides. Then fold down the top flap, add a loop and a button, and this unique and beautiful handbag is ready to use.

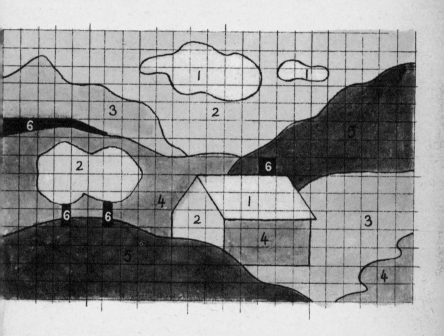

8. Weaving

WEAVING SQUARES

A household with children in it is quite likely to have a weaving frame or loom tucked away somewhere. Otherwise, you can buy or make one. Inexpensive looms are available in most toy shops or yarn stores. Most of them are adjustable in size, but this is not vital. If you can weave squares of 6″, 7″ or 8″, you can make any of the useful and attractive items in this chapter.

You can make a simple loom quite easily, if you prefer. You will need a rigid frame of smooth wood 6″ square (or any size you choose). Along this frame, at intervals of $\frac{1}{8}$″, hammer long thin brads so that they stand up evenly and firmly. That's all there is to it!

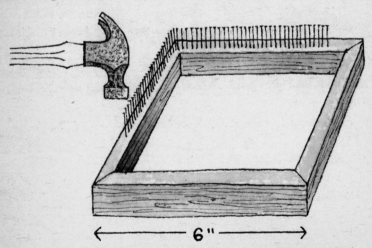

$\longleftarrow$ 6″ $\longrightarrow$

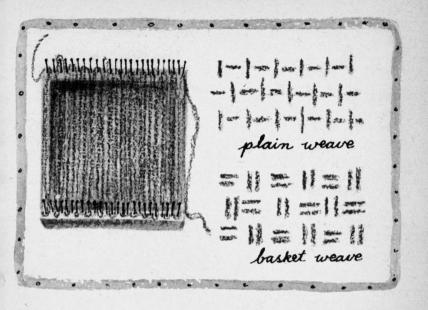

plain weave

basket weave

Weaving itself is a simple process which has been practiced since the beginning of time. Long before man learned to spin thread from cotton or wool, primitive peoples were weaving grasses and plant fibres into mats and fabrics.

The threads which run lengthwise, or vertically, in a woven fabric are called the warp. These threads go onto the loom first.

The threads which run crosswise are called the woof. They are also known as filling-in threads, as they fill in the warp.

Start your square by running a thread back and forth from top to bottom, winding it around each tooth of the loom. Next you will have to calculate how much yarn you need for the warp. If the warp is to be all of

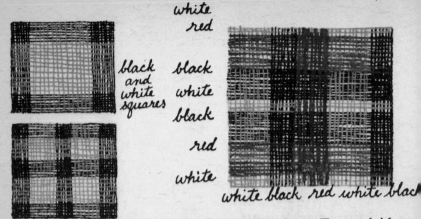

white
red
black
white
black
red
white

black
and
white
squares

white black red white blac[k]

one color, the one thread will be quite long. For a plaid pattern, you will need a number of shorter pieces. To get the exact amount, multiply the number of inches by the number of teeth to the inch, and then add a few extra inches for good measure. Use a crochet hook or a ribbon to pull weave the woof back and forth across the warp.

For plain weaving you go over one thread and under the next all across each row. You will probably use this weave most of the time. However, in addition to plain weaving there are many other weaves which give different effects. For instance, for the basket weave you go over two and under two, for the first two rows. Then for the next two rows you do just the opposite: under two, then over two.

You can experiment with all different kinds of weaves and work out diagonal effects, herringbones and chevrons. You should also experiment with color effects in plain weave—border patterns, checks and plaids which you achieve by changing colors in both the warp and the woof. You will find all sorts of uses for these experimental squares. A few suggestions follow.

THINGS TO MAKE FROM SINGLE SQUARES

Figuring out weaving patterns on paper is a good idea but you will soon discover that the only real way to find out how a certain weave or pattern of colors is going to look is to weave it! It is especially important before starting on a large project requiring many squares joined together. So, give free rein to your creative instincts and weave a whole selection of sample squares, for none of them will go to waste. You can turn each one into a useful little gift or use it to enhance something else.

EYEGLASS CASE: follow the directions for the tapestry eyeglass case on page 85.

TISSUE-HANKY CASE· same as eyeglass case, but leave the long side open instead of the narrow end.

POCKETS: Simply stitch one or two squares on to a dress, blouse or skirt, leaving the top open.

DOILY for dressing table.

HEAD and ARM RESTS for a chair.

MAT for under a vase or flower pot.

Wrapped around cardboard cylinder, to carry rolled-up paper, maps, drawings or posters to school.

POT HOLDER

A single square of plain weave, with the addition only of a loop for hanging, becomes a wonderful little pot holder if you make it of a heavy enough material. In craft stores, you can buy a sort of yarn which is actually a knitted tube of cotton, and this is ideal for pot holders. You can also use colorful rags if you prepare them first by cutting the cloth into bias strips one inch wide and then piecing the strips together lengthwise. You have to twist the strip as you work.

The important thing about a pot holder is to weave it properly so that it will be extremely tight and firm. Otherwise the person who is using it will burn her fingers, and that is what a pot holder is supposed to prevent!

Here are some ideas for various patterns:

Solid color to match the kitchen.

One color for the warp, another for the woof.

Outside border (use one color for first and last inch of warp and also for first and last inch of woof, and a second color for the rest).

Checkered pattern of 9, 12, 16 or 25 squares (alternate bands of two colors for both warp and woof).

Plaid (work out a pattern, using two or more colors, and involving just the woof, or both warp and woof).

SECRET WARMER

When winter winds blow, and the mercury drops out of sight, no one enjoys piling on one garment after another, but it's better than shivering and freezing. You can eliminate some of this bulk and still keep warm if you make yourself a woolly warmer to hide inside your winter coat.

The warmer is a little thing—only about 12″ to 15″ by 18″ to 24″, depending on how big you are—but it makes a surprising difference. It goes into your coat across your upper back and shoulder blades, and its additional warmth at this strategic area is equal to another whole garment!

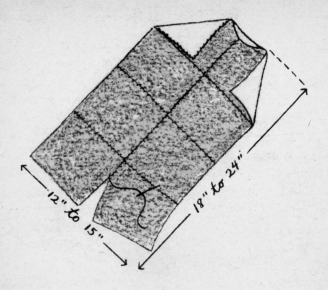

12" to 15"

18" to 24"

If your coat is open at the bottom, you can fasten the warmer in place with small safety pins between the lining and the outer part of the coat, and no one will be the wiser. Otherwise, you can match it to the lining of your coat, and pin or tack it in place on the inside of your coat or jacket.

Weave 6 squares or rectangles of heavy wool yarn to the necessary size and sew them together loosely so they will lie flat. Fold over flaps on the dotted lines to fit along the armholes, according to the illustration. Perfect weaving is unimportant, especially if the warmer is to go between coat and lining, so this is a good project for a beginner to practice on.

DOLL'S BLANKET

You can delight a little girl with a woven blanket for her dolly, or the little girl herself can embark on this simple project. This is a good way to use up sample squares that you have woven for practice, or when you were experimenting with different weaves or colors. You will need only 6 squares for a small blanket.

If you have no squares and wish to weave them especially for the doll's blanket, work 3 in pink and white and 3 in blue and white and assemble them in a checkerboard pattern. Or, work 4 squares in one color and 2 in another to make stripes. Using a simple overcast stitch, sew the squares together loosely so that the blanket will lie flat.

If your dolly needs a larger blanket, you will have to weave more squares or larger squares. If you want a blanket measuring 18″ × 24″ you will need 12 squares of 6″ each. You can work them in a checkerboard pattern, or make 10 squares of one color (or color combination) to form the border of the blanket, and 2 of another color for the middle of the blanket.

BABY BLANKETS

There is always a special joy in producing a hand-made gift for a new baby. Baby will need lots of blankets when he arrives, some small and others quite large. Give yourself plenty of time if you plan to weave a crib blanket, so that it will surely be ready when baby arrives. All of these blankets are made of small woven squares sewn together to form a block of the desired size.

RECEIVING BLANKET

A receiving blanket for a new baby should be square in shape. It requires 36 squares and will measure anywhere from 36″ to 48″ depending on the size of your loom. For instance, if you weave 7″ squares, the blanket will measure 42″ square. With 6″ squares you will produce a 36″ blanket. Of course, if you want a 48″ blanket made of 6″ squares, a little arithmetic shows that you will need 64 squares; the blanket will be 8 squares by 8 squares.

White, pink or pale blue are the best colors for a receiving blanket. Combine white with pink or white with blue, but keep to simple, quiet effects which will flatter the baby.

CARRIAGE COVER

A carriage cover should be approximately $36'' \times 42''$ in size. Figure out how many squares to weave according to the size of your individual squares.

You can weave the squares for a carriage cover of pastel shades combined with white in plaids or in a tweedy effect (as described on page 96). However, if you are making a carriage cover for a city baby, a dark shade will be appropriate because it is so much more practical. Choose navy blue, hunter green or a dark grey and, if you care to, bind the edge in matching grosgrain ribbon for a neat, tailored effect.

CRIB BLANKET

Most ambitious project of all is a crib blanket, but this makes an impressive gift, and one which will give years of usefulness.

You can choose from a wide range of colors, for almost any color which is not too intense will make an attractive blanket. Yellow or pale green are especially nice, and will safely get you past the hurdle of the traditional "pink-for-a-girl and blue-for-a-boy" guessing game.

You can have fun working out a pattern of your own, or choose one from those illustrated here. You can make the squares of random plaid using white and one other pastel color, or white plus two other colors, say pink and blue. Or you can make the blanket of a solid color or an all-over tweed effect (like the afghan on page 108).

The blanket should be approximately 42″ × 60″ in size. Bind the edges with nylon, satin or sateen blanket binding for greater durability.

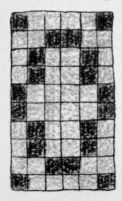 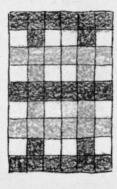 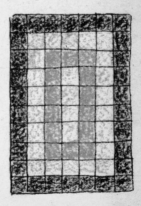

TWEEDY AFGHAN

Making an afghan, whether you crochet it, knit it or weave it, is a long-term project, but a very rewarding one. A handsome afghan looks beautiful thrown over the back of a couch, where it is always handy when you need it. It will give years—and even generations—of pleasure!

This afghan is woven a square at a time and then assembled. A great advantage of making an afghan this way is that the loom is small enough to carry about with you, so that you can work at odd times and fill in many a moment pleasantly which otherwise would have been wasted.

There is no specific "right size" for an afghan, and the exact size of one assembled from squares depends in part upon the size of the squares themselves. Let us say that your loom produces 6″ squares. You can make an afghan 48″ × 54″ by assembling 72 such squares in 8 rows of 9 squares each. You can get an afghan of almost the same size with 8″ squares, using only 42 squares arranged in 6 rows of 7 each. The afghan will actually measure 48″ × 56″ in size.

To produce an attractive tweedy effect you simply use one color yarn for the warp and another for filling in the woof. A combination of two shades of one color— two yellows, for example, or two shades of dusty pink— gives a very pleasing effect. Also interesting is a combination of two different cool colors, such as a blue and a green, or a purple or a blue; or two warm shades, such as orange and red, or red and yellow. Make a few sample squares in different combinations till you find

one you like, and note how much yarn the sample square uses, so that you can estimate how much to buy for the entire afghan.

Make all the squares of your afghan the same for a beautiful, conservative effect. If you would like a somewhat bolder afghan, while still maintaining the tweedy effect, make half the squares of a cool combination and the other half of a warm combination, and sew them together in a checkerboard pattern. For instance, a bright, gay afghan for a young person's room might combine squares in two shades of red with squares in two shades of blue. Or, for a striking, sophisticated afghan, combine squares in white and pale grey with squares of black and dark grey.

When you have woven enough squares for one row, sew them together into a strip so that they won't get lost. Overcast them loosely so that they will lie flat and smooth, with no puckers. When all the strips are finished, sew them together. For greater durability and to enhance the afghan still further, bind the edges with satin or velvet ribbon for an added note of luxury.

9. Bag and Baggage

LUGGAGE IDENTIFIERS

Every now and then you find some simple gadget which is worth its weight in gold because it eliminates one of the annoying complications of our modern lives. Here is just such an item for the person who travels by plane or train: a set of identical, bright-colored, easy-to-see luggage identifiers.

They make a wonderful going-away present for the person who "has everything"—and no more room inside his luggage anyway! He will bless you every time he assembles his luggage quickly, and if he is in a foreign country where he doesn't speak the language, he will be able to get a porter to collect his luggage merely by showing a sample of the yarn and using sign language!

The gadget itself is nothing more than a braid with tassels at each end. You tie one to the handle of each piece of baggage. For each identifier, braid 9 strands of yarn, 12″ long, and tie the ends. Attach a small tassel (see page 61) to each end. Use one or more bright, sharp colors (especially good are the fluorescent colors) which you can spot at a glance. Make one for each suitcase, plus a few extras for additional luggage or bundles which may be acquired en route, but be sure to make each set uniform!

MORE IDENTIFIER IDEAS

Did you ever read about two strangers who arrange to meet, each wearing a red carnation so that they will know each other? Objects are even harder to identify than people, and nowadays so many things are mass-produced, it is often difficult to find our own belongings among many almost identical ones. This is true not only in public places, but even at home. Solve the problem with your own special set of identifiers in some distinctive color, or a combination of colors such as one purple tassel and one orange, and use them for any of the following:

Bicycle
Baby buggy
Ice skates
Car—tie on to the radio antenna to spot
      your car easily when parked
School bag
Raincoat
Lunchbox
Umbrella
Various items of sports equipment
Toys, such as sand bucket, digging spade, etc.

Remember that the identifier needn't stay on at all times, but just when the item is "parked" with others of its kind. Even a man's dark overcoat, amidst a pile of similar ones on the host's bed during a party, can be temporarily marked and easily found if it wears a distinctive identifier.

BEACH BAG

What could be handier than a beach bag which lets you see what you are looking for? This bag will keep you in the swim when you carry your towels and swimsuit. A special feature is the separate but attached purse for small items.

First, cut out two circles, each 12″ in diameter, from the sturdy sections of an old raincoat or shower curtain. Sandwich a round of cardboard, cut to the same size, between them. Make holes around the edge at one-inch intervals and about ½″ in from the edge, using a hole puncher. Better still, put in grommets (metal eyelets) with an inexpensive gadget you can buy for just that purpose.

Through each eyelet, run a strand of heavy cotton yarn or string, 30″ long, and tie each strand to the eyelet so that two ends dangle down, each 15″ long. Now proceed to knot the strands exactly as you did for the

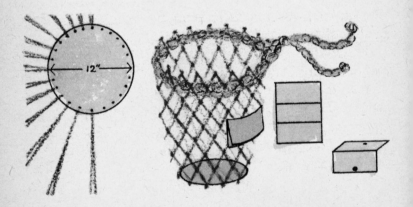

String Shopping Bag on page 76, but continue knotting to the very ends of the strands.

A drawstring goes through the top of the bag, in and out of the final loops. Take 2 yards of cotton rope and knot it at the middle. Draw it through the loops, going twice round the bag, and knot the ends together.

To complete the bag, make an envelope out of a rectangle of the plastic, 6″ by 15″, following the illustration. Finish the envelope with a snapper for closing, and stitch it on the outside of the bag for money, keys and other small items which would otherwise slip through the fringe.

10. Gifts for Men

Among the hardest types of gifts to find are those for men. It's always good to have an idea or two up your sleeve, especially for gifts which you can make lovingly for someone special. By the same token, items for men sell well at bazaars and fund-raising fairs.

DESK SAVER

A cylindrical cardboard carton, such as oatmeal sometimes comes in, will serve as the basis for a gift certain to be appreciated by any man (or woman for that matter) who uses a desk. A tall tin can whose lid has been smoothly removed, so as to leave no rough edges, can be used instead.

Paint the outside of the cylinder with a gummy paste, such as rubber cement, or give it a coat of shellac, from the top to about half way down. Now start winding yarn—wool or cotton—from the top down, keeping each twist as close as possible to the one above it. When you reach the end of the sticky part, coat the lower half with glue and continue winding down to the bottom.

The desk saver will hold pens and pencils, rulers and compasses, scissors and even booklets. It will help the man in your life keep the desk in his life safe from clutter.

CLOSET GADGETS

There are lots of things you can make out of lengths of ordinary braid, or horse reins made with a spool (see page 30), to keep a man's possessions neat and orderly. Here are some ideas for his closet:

TIE HOLDER: Wrap braid around the lower rung of a wooden coat hanger and it will make an excellent tie rack.

SHOE RACK: For each pair of shoes you need two 10″ lengths of braid. Nail the ends of the braid to the base-board of the closet, or to a board which you will attach to the wall of the closet. The ends of each braid should be 3″ apart.

UMBRELLA HOLDER: Loop a 6″ length of braid to the jamb of the closet just inside the door.

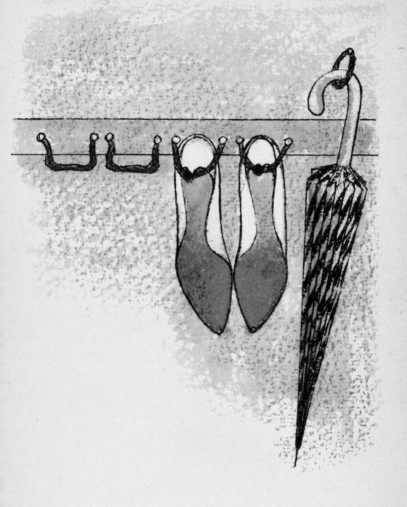

WORKSHOP GADGETS

TOOL HOLDER: Just 6″ above the top of the workbench is the place for a woolly tool holder. Nail the braid to the wall every few inches, leaving some slack between nails. The longer your braid, the more tools can be handily stowed away, ready for use.

NAIL BOXES: Take four or six wooden match boxes, the kind that slide in and out like drawers. Glue them together according to the illustration and then coat the top, bottom and sides with glue. Wrap yarn around and around until those surfaces are completely covered. Use a bit of yarn to sew a small ring to the front of each drawer for a handle.

SHOESHINE SHAGGY

You will shine in the eyes of a man if you give him a shaggy shiner for his shoes. Start with a piece of heavy flannel or a piece of soft woollen or jersey cloth about $4'' \times 20''$. Next make 72 very small tassels (see page 61) of the softest wool yarn you have. Make the tassels around a piece of cardboard only $\frac{1}{2}''$ or $\frac{3}{4}''$ wide.

Sew the tassels to the shoe shiner close together in 8 rows of 9 tassels each. They go heads down, fringe side out, at the middle of the cloth, according to the illustration. Both sides of the shining cloth are usable, but the shoe shiner should end up by shining the shoes with the lintless tassel side of the cloth.

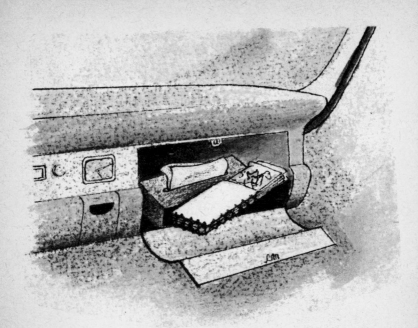

ROAD MAP FILE

They say you can tell what a woman is like from looking at her top bureau drawer, and perhaps the same thing holds for men. You can judge their character by the condition of the dashboard compartment or the side pocket in the car that holds maps. A file that holds maps in neat readiness is a great morale builder on the open road. Here is one that you can make in a minimum of time, for a maximum of usefulness.

For materials you can use any one of a variety of materials. Cardboard, felt or canvas will do, or heavy plastic upholstery fabric, or even real leather such as you might salvage from an old pocketbook which has gone at the edges. You will need two pieces, one $4'' \times 5''$ and the other $4'' \times 7''$.

Make perforations around the two long sides and one short side of the smaller piece, at intervals of $\frac{1}{2}''$ and $\frac{1}{4}''$ in from the edge. Use this as a stencil to mark dots on the larger piece and perforate the dots.

You will need very heavy yarn, or a double strand of yarn, to work the two pieces together. Place a block about $4'' \times 4'' \times \frac{1}{2}''$ between the two pieces of fabric so that the pocket will be roomy enough to hold several maps, and weave the edges together through the holes. Go around once in one direction and a second time in the opposite direction.

INDEX